THE LEADERSHIP CHALLENGE® VISION BOOK

James M. Kouzes & Barry Z. Posner
with Dan Schwab

Pfeiffer
A Wiley Imprint
www.pfeiffer.com

Published by Pfeiffer
An Imprint of Wiley
989 Market Street
San Francisco, CA 94103-1741
www.pfeiffer.com

ISBN: 978-0-470-59203-8

Acquiring Editor: Lisa Shannon
Director of Development: Kathleen Dolan Davies
Development Editor: Janis Fisher Chan
Production Editor: Dawn Kilgore
Editor: Rebecca Taff
Manufacturing Supervisor: Becky Morgan
Design: izles design

Printed in the United States of America

Printing   10 9 8 7 6 5 4 3 2 1

CONTENTS

HOW TO USE THIS WORKBOOK

Most of us want to leave the world better than we found it. We strive to change and improve things so that our children's world is richer and more equitable than our own.

We have dreams of a better future, one in which our aspirations become more completely realized than they are now. If you have such a dream of the future, or would like to develop one, this workbook is for you.

The following pages are meant to help you look ahead and envision a better state of affairs for your family, for your team, for your organization, for your community. And once you have a better picture of that ideal future in mind, we will help you to communicate it more effectively to those who can help you implement it.

In addition, this workbook contains sections that will help you make your team a more forward-thinking group and your organization a more visionary place. And because visions are co-created and shared, there is a section on how to build visionary skills in others.

Finally, because all leadership is self-development, there is a section with practical activities you can use to become a more competent visionary yourself.

Though these materials are presented in a sequence, don't feel bound by it. Each exercise is here because it adds something to your overall skills as a leader—but you can engage the exercises in any way that is useful for you. So if you need to present a vision to your group soon, start with "develop and deliver a vision." If you have more time, you might consider starting with some of the self-development exercises that follow.

Each section contains activities to help you focus on the skills needed to become more adept at looking ahead and creating the workplace and the world you would like to see. Many pages are designed to be reproduced so that you can use them as worksheets to help you become more adept as a vision practitioner. Each of these pages is identified as such in the footer.

For those who have participated in *The Leadership Challenge® Workshop*, much of the framework that underlies this workbook has already been presented to you. We recap the highlights of this information on the following pages. If you have not been through the workshop, then more information on the concepts is to be found in *The Leadership Challenge* chapters on Inspire a Shared Vision.

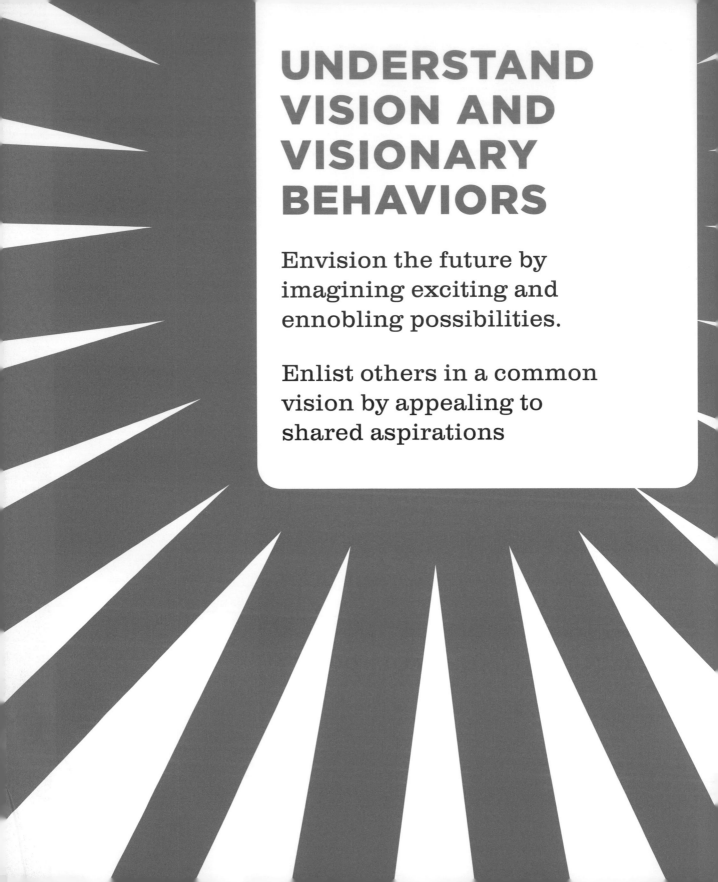

UNDERSTAND VISION AND VISIONARY BEHAVIORS

Envision the future by imagining exciting and ennobling possibilities.

Enlist others in a common vision by appealing to shared aspirations

What Is Vision?

We define vision as:

An IDEAL and UNIQUE IMAGE of the FUTURE for the COMMON GOOD

This means that to be effective, a vision must:

- Speak of a desired future state of affairs

- Aspire to a high standard

- Be tailored to a specific situation

- Build on values—what is most important to you and to others

- Engage the aspirations of your audience

- Use visual imagery

- Motivate people to action

In addition, the practice of Inspire a Shared Vision has two key components or commitments:

1. **Envision the future** by imagining exciting and ennobling possibilities

2. **Enlist others** in a common vision by appealing to shared aspirations

As you consider this definition of vision and the two commitments associated with it, reflect on the following questions:

1. **What do you think when you hear the words "envision the future"?** What does this mean to you?

- -
· ·
- -
· ·
- -
· ·

2. **Have you ever felt you had a vision?** If so, what became of it? If not, what might you gain if you had one?

- -
· ·
- -
· ·

3. **What is the distinction between the mission of your organization and your vision for it?**

- -
· ·
- -
· ·
- -
· ·
- -

4. When you consider the phrase "enlist others in a common vision," what comes to mind? What does this mean to you? Why is "enlisting others" important?

....

....

....

5. Why are "shared aspirations" important?

....

....

• • • • • • • • • • • • • •

Behaviors Associated with Inspire a Shared Vision

These are the six behaviors specific to Inspire a Shared Vision. The number next to each refers to the position of these behaviors among the thirty behaviors of leadership measured by the LPI.

LPI ITEM #2   I talk about future trends that will influence how our work gets done.

LPI ITEM #7   I describe a compelling image of what our future could be like.

LPI ITEM #12   I appeal to others to share an exciting dream of the future.

LPI ITEM #17   I show others how their long-term interests can be realized by enlisting in a common vision.

LPI ITEM #22   I paint the "big picture" of what we aspire to accomplish.

LPI ITEM #27   I speak with genuine conviction about the higher meaning and purpose of our work.

The *Leadership Practices Inventory* was designed as an instrument to help you understand the behavioral aspect of leadership—those things leaders *do* that the rest of us see as effective and willingly follow.

As you revisit your LPI Feedback Report, answer the following questions. (If you have not completed the LPI, you can rate yourself on how frequently you engage in each behavior using a 1 to 10 scale, with 1 indicating "Almost Never" and 10 being "Almost Always." See the Resources section for more information on how to access and use this instrument.)

1. **What do these statements mean to you?** How or why is each significant?

....

....

2. **How do you interpret your scores?** Where are your strengths now? Which of these behaviors are "common practice" for you, either in your eyes or in the experience of those around you?

....

....

3. **Where do you already know you can improve the frequency of engaging in these behaviors?**

....

....

GET BETTER AT *THE VISION THING*

Leadership is a personal endeavor. The number one thing we look for in a leader is credibility—that quality of being authentic, of having belief, word and action in alignment.

Enhance Your Vision Skills

The *Leadership Practices Inventory* provides a wealth of data about your current practice of the six behaviors related to Inspire a Shared Vision.

Use the following methods to delve deeper into these skills and to increase the *frequency* with which you use them.

1. **Choose the vision behavior that had the highest score from your observers.** This indicates an area of strength for you. Were you aware of this? Make an inventory of how you think you exhibit this behavior. What can you do to be even stronger here?

....

....
----

2. **Choose one of your two lowest rated behaviors.** People see you engaging in this activity less frequently. What would you gain if people around you saw you demonstrating this behavior more frequently?

....

....

3. How might you increase the frequency of this behavior?

....

....

----

4. What resources might help you build strength with all six vision behaviors?

....

....

● ● ● ● ● ● ● ● ● ● ● ● ● ● ●

Learn More About the Visionary in You

The following two exercises will help you to broaden your personal horizons, providing a stronger base from which to think of vision for your team, your organization, and your community.

Exercise 1: Your Past as Prologue

Surprising as it may sound, research has shown that the more understanding a person has of his or her past, the better able he or she is to predict the future. The more that we appreciate the themes in our own lives, the more able we are to plot a future course that is consistent with our values and principles.

Our own lives are often our best teachers, particularly when it comes to leadership—to understanding what motivates us, what our preferences and beliefs are, what our natural strengths are, what moves us to action or change, what helps us succeed and what gets in the way, and what we strive for in our lives and in our work.

In this exercise you will look back at significant experiences in your work and personal life to see what they can teach you about the person you are and the leader you can become.

Becoming more adept as one who can conceive of and deliver vision requires considerable knowledge of self.

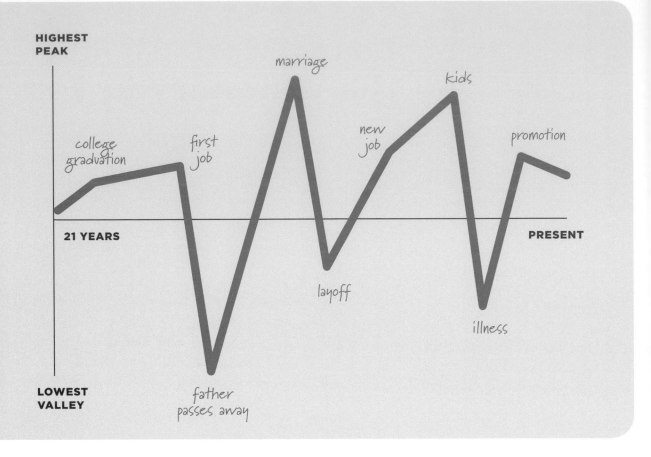

INSTRUCTIONS

Create a grid on the following page similar to the one above, and then spend a few minutes charting the **significant events or experiences** in your life, starting at age 21 and continuing to the present.

- Focus primarily on your work life, but don't neglect important events in your personal life.

- If the event or experience was a "peak," plot it above the line; if it was a "valley," plot it below the line.

- Some "peaks" will be higher than others, and some "valleys" will be lower than others.

- Next to each event or experience you plot, jot down a few notes to identify it.

**HIGHEST
PEAK**

21 YEARS

PRESENT

**LOWEST
VALLEY**

THEN ANSWER THE FOLLOWING QUESTIONS:

1. Is there a theme or pattern to the peaks in your "life line"? What does this consist of?

- -

. . . .

- -

. . . .

- -

2. If there is a theme or pattern to the valleys, what is it?

- -

. . . .

- -

. . . .

- -

3. What helped you get out of the valleys in your past?

- -

. . . .

- -

. . . .

- -

4. What does your life line tell you about who you are as a leader and what matters most to you?

. . . .

. . . .

----

5. How might you incorporate these insights into a vision you are creating for your team or organization?

. . . .

. . . .

Exercise 2:
Envision Your Future

A useful component of envisioning the future of your organization is to think hard about where **you** are going. An honest exploration of your personal vision will give credibility to any vision in which you wish to involve others.

1. If you could lead anything, what would it be?

....

----

2. Where do you see yourself in five years? What will you be doing, and with whom?

....

....

3. What is your ideal personal future?

....

....

....

Leadership is a personal endeavor. The number one thing we look for in a leader is credibility—that quality of being authentic, of having belief, word, and action in alignment.

4. **Picture the party to celebrate your retirement after a long and distinguished career.** Who will be there? What will people be saying about you?

. . . .

. . . .

. . . .

5. **What legacy would you like to leave to your company, your family, and your community?**

. . . .

. . . .

. . . .

DEVELOP AND DELIVER A VISION

Creating a vision starts with knowing what you want to do or where you want to go and then applying the skills of Inspire a Shared Vision to refining and delivering that message.

Create a Message

1. **What do I want my/our future to be?** What will it look like? Who will be there? What will we be doing?

....

....

As you begin shaping your vision, ask yourself these questions.

2. **What would "an exciting dream of the future" look like?**

....

....

3. **What is the meaning of the future I want to create?** What values does it express? What larger purpose will we be serving?

....

....

----

4. What do I know about the trends and influences that will shape the future I want to create? What do I need to research in order to be better informed?

....

....

This is a thoughtful process; take as much time as you need to formulate answers that are meaningful to you and to others.

5. Who will be affected by my vision? What is important to them? How will they benefit?

....

....

----

6. How can I be sure to take this from **my** vision to **our** vision?

....

....

....

7. How does my vision reflect and tie into a larger vision of the future in our organization?

....

....

8. How can I create a "big picture" image of the future that appeals to others?

....

....

....

Know Your Constituents

Building a compelling vision of the future that will motivate others to action requires that you investigate the needs and aspirations of your audience. Use these questions as a starting point for assessing the dreams and goals of your constituents.

Make duplicates of this worksheet for each person who will be affected by your vision of the future. Given the personal nature of vision, you might be better served to make this assessment by interviewing each person, using the following pages for notes.

Vision Worksheet

1. **Where do you see yourself in five years?** If you could be doing what you *really* want to do, what would that look like?

. . . .

. . . .

2. **When it comes down to it, what matters most to you?**

. . . .

. . . .

3. **Where do you see our organization in three to five years?** What will we be doing? What will it be like to work here?

. . . .

. . . .

NAME:

The Leadership Challenge® Workshop, Fourth Edition. Copyright © 2010 by James M. Kouzes and Barry Z. Posner. Reproduced by permission of Pfeiffer, an Imprint of Wiley. www.pfeiffer.com.

4. **In what direction do you see our organization evolving?** Where would you have us go?

. . . .

. . . .

----

6. **How can I involve you in co-creating the future?** What is your dream?

. . . .

. . . .

Craft Your Vision Presentation

Indeed, choosing the most effective language, metaphors, and imagery is an art. Consider the techniques Dr. Martin Luther King, Jr., used that made his "I Have a Dream" speech so effective. Adapt these techniques to make the *delivery* of your vision as compelling as the *ideas* it contains.

Having a clear vision in your own mind doesn't bring it into being—you must communicate effectively so that others "catch" your vision from you.

LANGUAGE AND IMAGERY

1. What specific language can I use to convey my ideas to others?

. . . .

. . . .

2. What imagery can I use that will convey a powerful mental picture to my audience?

. . . .

. . . .

----

3. What metaphors and symbols will be evocative for people listening to me?

_____

· ·

_____

· ·

4. What jargon should I avoid?

_____

· ·

_____

· ·

5. How can I make sure that my language clearly states that this is **our** vision and not just **my** vision?

_____

· ·

_____

· ·

_____

CREATE VERSIONS OF YOUR VISION SPEECH

As you consider each constituent group you will present to, create a version of your presentation suitable to that audience. Make note of what is different in each situation and how you would adapt your overall message to suit.

Consider creating versions of your presentation that address differences such as these:

- Presenting to different groups, such as a finance team, an engineering group, a project team, or to senior executives

- A speech to be delivered in a formal setting in front of a large group

- An "elevator speech" of two minutes or less

- An informal version suitable for "water cooler" conversations

- A concise written version that could be inserted into a strategic plan or other document

TEST YOUR VISION PRESENTATION

Test a draft of your vision by voicing it to a trusted colleague. It is useful to hear yourself articulate the vision, as well to obtain feedback on what the other person heard. Seek constructive criticism on both the **content** and the **style** of your presentation.

Avoid reading your presentation or it may come across as stiff and formal. Most opportunities to share vision are conversational. Get some conversational practice before you work with a larger audience.

CHOOSE YOUR PRESENTATION VENUE

Consider when and where you will present your vision to a given group. What can you do to create an atmosphere most conducive for conveying your message?

To be effective, you will have to deliver your vision to people in different settings and circumstances.

Draft Your Vision Statement

Use the ideas you recorded on the previous pages to create a draft of your vision presentation.

Evaluate Your Vision Presentation

1. How effective was I in conveying "a unique ideal image of the future for the common good"?

_____

....

_____

2. Did my vision come across as inspiring?

_____

....

_____

As you reflect on the experience of giving your presentation to others, ask yourself:

3. How else could I adjust the content of my presentation?

_____

....

_____

....

_____

....

_____

4. **Did the presentation of my vision actually come out the way I intended it to?** Where did my delivery best match the intention of my ideas? Where was it awkward?

....

....

5. **How did people react to what I said, and to how I said it?**

....

----

6. **What will I do differently next time?**

....

....

7. **What did I learn from this experience?**

....

....

Seek Feedback from Others

Distribute copies of the feedback form on the next page and ask others to complete it after hearing your vision presentation.

Vision Presentation Feedback Form

As you listen to my presentation, please make notes to help me improve my ability to deliver on this important skill.

MESSAGE

1. What did you get from what I said? If you had to distill my message down to two or three key points, what would they be?

....

....

----

2. Was the content of my message suitable to the context of the situation? Did anything seem out of place? What other ideas might I have added?

....

....

NAME (optional):

DELIVERY

1. In conveying my message, what did I do effectively that you would suggest I continue to do?

....

....

....

2. What could I do differently that would help me to better articulate my message, both to myself and to you? How can I better express a genuine conviction about the meaning of the direction I think we should go?

....

....

....

STRENGTHEN YOUR SKILLS AS A VISIONARY

Research has shown that vision skills are among the hardest to learn of all leadership behaviors. Use these practical exercises to help you develop your "vision muscles."

Continue to Craft Your Vision Message

DEEPEN YOUR CONVICTION

Continue to delve into your own motivation about the future. What are you most excited about?

USE OUTSIGHT

Envisioning a future that takes your team/organization beyond where it is now requires a large frame of reference. Research areas of knowledge relevant to where you think your team/organization is going. Look outside your normal "boundaries" for new and innovative ways to think about the future.

USE A MIND MAP

Mind mapping is a popular and time-tested form of brainstorming. Mind maps are a way to organize one's thoughts around a central idea. Essentially, one creates a diagram of all the associated thoughts and begins to draw connections between the thoughts, which results in development and clarity of the central idea. It is often conducted on paper, but there are also many online resources available for mind mapping. Search on mind map or mind mapping.

BUILD A TIMELINE

Developing the ideas that form the core of your vision takes time. Create a time map of the steps you need to complete to build your vision presentation.

● ● ● ● ● ● ● ● ● ● ● ● ● ● ● ●

Refine the Delivery of Your Vision

JOIN A PRESENTATION CLASS OR CLUB

To strengthen your comfort with public speaking, take a class from Toastmaster's or enroll in a presentation skills class.

FIND OPPORTUNITIES TO SPEAK IN PUBLIC

Seek out opportunities that allow you to speak in front of others. At work, volunteer to present at meetings. In your community, get involved with groups that provide you an audience.

LISTEN TO MOTIVATING SPEECHES BY OTHERS

Seek out examples of well-written and effectively delivered speeches and presentations. What makes them work? What techniques are the presenters using?

INTERVIEW A SPEECHWRITER

Find someone in your community who writes speeches and presentations for a living. Do an interview to find out his or her "best practices."

BUILD VISIONARY TEAMS AND ORGANIZATIONS

You are unlikely to achieve your vision by acting alone. Engage your colleagues in an ongoing discovery of the unique, ideal future you want to create together.

Being visionary is hard work. Many of us have very little experience in consciously nurturing these skills. You can affect this situation by thoughtfully interjecting "vision enhancing" activities into your organization—be it your immediate work team or even the entire company.

The following suggestions provide ways you can strengthen your organization to be "forward-looking" and to build momentum in others to create a future worthy of your organization's past.

Consider employing any of the following ideas with your team or work group. For each, identify a specific person, team, or situation to apply it to.

- Make a "futures report" a regular part of staff meeting agendas.

- Create a "futures department" dedicated to tracking issues affecting your organization.

- Develop a process for forecasting future trends that affect your industry.

- Circulate journals from future-oriented organizations.

- Create a book club whose focus is on future-oriented thinking.

- Bring in thinkers from outside your industry to talk about trends their organizations are dealing with.

- Host a "futures fair" that highlights new developments taking place across your organization or industry.

BUILD VISIONARY CAPACITY IN OTHERS

One of the greatest gifts you can give people around you is the recognition that they too can become visionaries. Use these suggestions to consciously build visionary skills in others—inside your organization or in your community.

ASSIGN PROJECTS THAT HAVE A FUTURE COMPONENT TO THEM

Consciously design job assignments that require the people doing them to look ahead and uncover the need for forecasting future developments.

Individuals:

....

Ideas:

....

BUILD FUTURE ORIENTATION INTO PERFORMANCE REVIEWS

Make the assessment of your direct reports' abilities to be forward-looking part of their annual reviews.

Individuals:

....

Ideas:

....

For each idea, list particular individuals you could use it with and specific activities or assignments you could have them do.

PROVIDE MENTORSHIP OPPORTUNITIES

Pair people up with leaders in your organization who can help them learn higher-order skills. This will encourage them to "think big" about their own visions of the organization and their places in it.

Individuals:

- -

. . . .

Ideas:

- -

. . . .

- -

ENCOURAGE COMPETENCE IN PRESENTATION SKILLS

Speaking with confidence in public is of tremendous importance in the workplace. Help your colleagues find ways to increase their skills through training and chances to practice.

Individuals:

- -

. . . .

Ideas:

- -

. . . .

- -

ENCOURAGE A DIALOG

Find opportunities to keep an open discussion going with members of your staff about trends shaping your organization.

Individuals:

- -

. . . .

Ideas:

- -

. . . .

- -

EVALUATE THE RESULTS OF VISION

The purpose of vision is to create positive change in the world. Evaluate the effect you are having by being more intentional in expressing your image of the future.

Vision Implementation Evaluation Form

Use this worksheet periodically to evaluate progress on implementing your vision.

1. The main points I was trying to convey were:

. . . .

. . . .

----

2. Evidence that the vision is showing results includes:

. . . .

. . . .

3. Where I don't see anything happening:

. . . .

. . . .

THE TOPIC OF MY VISION WAS (project):

I CONVEYED IT TO (constituents):

ON (date):

4. Given the above analysis, this is how I would evaluate the results of my vision to date:

....

----

5. How do I need to adapt my message given recent changes elsewhere in our organization?

....

....

I WILL PRESENT THIS REVISED VERSION OF MY VISION TO (constituents):

ON (date):

6. I would restate my vision now as follows:

....

....

7. Who else in the organization might I involve in order to strengthen the impact of my vision?

....

Vision Presentation Follow-Up Feedback Form

In order to become more effective at expressing my vision of our future, I would appreciate your feedback.

1. What do you remember as the key points of the vision?

I PRESENTED YOU WITH MY VISION FOR (project):

ON (date):

2. Do you think of this as **my** vision or **our** vision?

---

3. What has happened since my presentation that is a result of the vision I presented?

---

4. What hasn't happened that you thought might?

. . . .

. . . .

5. What suggestions do you have for where we take this from here?

. . . .

. . . .

. . . .

The Leadership Challenge® Workshop, Fourth Edition. Copyright © 2010 by James M. Kouzes and Barry Z. Posner. Reproduced by permission of Pfeiffer, an Imprint of Wiley. www.pfeiffer.com.

RESOURCES FOR INSPIRE A SHARED VISION

You are not alone in your journey to envision a better world. Learn from others to deepen your skills and model them for others.

SUGGESTIONS FOR IMPROVING YOUR PRACTICE OF INSPIRE A SHARED VISION

- Become a futurist. Join the World Futures Society. Read *American Demographics* or other magazines about future trends. Use the Internet to find a "futures" conference that you can attend. Make a list of what reputable people are predicting will happen in the next ten years.

- Every week, think of something you can do to clarify the kind of future you would like people to create together.

- Set up a process for looking ahead and forecasting future trends.

- Constantly look for ways in which you can get input from others on your vision, and encourage others to envision an uplifting and ennobling future.

- Keep a list of your constituents. Identify those you haven't reached out to yet and think about how you can learn more about their hopes and dreams.

- Set aside time at least once every month to talk about the future with your staff. Make your vision of the future part of a staff meeting, a working lunch, conversations by the water cooler, and so on.

- Read a biography of a visionary leader. Make notes about the way the person communicated vision and enlisted others in a common vision.

- Join Toastmasters or take a course in effective presentations to learn how to communicate your vision more effectively.

- Ask yourself, "Am I in the job to do something or am I in it for something to do?" Make a list of what you want to accomplish while you are in your current job—and why.

- Visualize what it will be like to attain your vision. Rehearse this scenario frequently in your mind.

- Read your vision speech to someone who will give you constructive feedback. Ask the person these questions: "Is the speech imaginative or conservative? Is it unique or ordinary? Does it evoke visual images? Is it oriented toward the future or toward the present? Does it offer a view that can be shared by others?"

- Hone your vision down to a short phrase of five to nine words that captures its essence.

- Regularly revisit and refine your vision. Think about events in the world, trends in your business, and changes in your life that might affect your vision.

- Look for CDs, tapes, podcasts, and videos of famous speeches by leaders who've inspired a shared vision. Learn everything you can from the masters. Keep a journal in which you note what you can use.

- Interview a speech writer. Ask him or her to share methods for constructing an inspirational speech.

- Read a book from the recommended list.

- Watch a movie from the recommended list for Inspire a Shared Vision, available at www.leadershipchallenge.com/go/videos.

SUGGESTED FURTHER READING ON INSPIRE A SHARED VISION

Boyd Clarke and Ron Crossland, *The Leader's Voice: How Your Communication Can Inspire Action and Get Results!* New York: Select Books, 2002.

Belle Linda Halpren and Kathy Lubar, *Leadership Presence: Dramatic Techniques to Reach Out, Motivate, and Inspire.* New York: Gotham Books, 2003.

Gary Hamel, *Leading the Revolution.* Boston: Harvard Business School Press, 2000.

Chip Heath and Don Heath, *Made to Stick: Why Some Ideas Survive and Others Die*. New York: Random House, 2007.

Jennifer James, *Thinking in the Future Tense: Leadership Skills for the New Age.* New York: Simon & Schuster, 1996.

Robert Johansen, *Leaders Make the Future: Ten New Leadership Skills for an Uncertain World*. San Francisco: Berrett-Koehler, 2009.

Matt Miller, *The Tyranny of Dead Ideas: Letting Go of the Old Ways of Thinking to Unleash a New Prospering*. New York: Henry Holt, 2009.

John Naisbitt, *Mindset: Eleven Ways to Change the Way You See—and Create—the Future.* New York: HarperCollins, 2006.

Burt Nanus, *Visionary Leadership.* San Francisco: Jossey-Bass, 1992.

Daniel H. Pink, *Drive: The Surprising Truth About What Motivates Us*. New York: Riverhead Books, 2009.

Bruce Sterling, *Tomorrow Now: Envisioning the Next Fifty Years.* New York: Random House, 2003.

Jim and Barry have received the American Society for Training and Development's highest award for Distinguished Contribution to Workplace Learning and Performance.

ABOUT THE AUTHORS

Jim Kouzes and Barry Posner are coauthors of the award-winning and best-selling book, The Leadership Challenge. This book was selected as one of the Top 10 books on leadership of all time (according to *The 100 Best Business Books of All Time*), won the James A. Hamilton Hospital Administrators' Book-of-the-Year Award and the Critics' Choice Award from the nation's book review editors, was a *Business Week* best-seller, and has sold over 1.8 million copies in more than twenty languages. Jim and Barry have coauthored more than a dozen other leadership books, including *A Leader's Legacy*—selected by *Soundview Executive Book Summaries* as one of the top thirty books of the year—*Credibility: How Leaders Gain It and Lose It, Why People Demand It*—chosen by *Industry Week* as one of its year's five best management books—*Encouraging the Heart*, *The Student Leadership Challenge*, and *The Academic Administrator's Guide to Exemplary Leadership*. They also developed the highly acclaimed *Leadership Practices Inventory* (LPI), a 360-degree questionnaire for assessing leadership behavior, which is one of the most widely used leadership assessment instruments in the world. More than four hundred doctoral dissertations and academic research projects have been based on the Five Practices of Exemplary Leadership® model.

Among the honors and awards that Jim and Barry have received are the Management/Leadership Educators of the Year by the International Management Council (this honor puts them in the company of Ken Blanchard, Stephen Covey, Peter Drucker, Edward Deming, Frances Hesselbein, Lee Iacocca, Rosabeth Moss Kanter, Norman Vincent Peale, and Tom Peters, who are all past recipients of the award); and named among the Top 50 Leadership Coaches in the nation (according to *Coaching for Leadership*).

Jim and Barry are frequent conference speakers, and each has conducted leadership development programs for hundreds of organizations, including Apple, Applied

Materials, ARCO, AT&T, Australia Post, Bank of America, Bose, Charles Schwab, Cisco Systems, Community Leadership Association, Conference Board of Canada, Consumers Energy, Dell Computer, Deloitte Touche, Dorothy Wylie Nursing Leadership Institute, Egon Zehnder International, Federal Express, Gymboree, Hewlett-Packard, IBM, Jobs DR-Singapore, Johnson & Johnson, Kaiser Foundation Health Plans and Hospitals, L. L. Bean, Lawrence Livermore National Labs, Lucile Packard Children's Hospital, Merck, Mervyn's, Motorola, NetApp, Northrop Grumman, Roche Bioscience, Siemens, Standard Aero, Sun Microsystems, 3M, Toyota, the U.S. Postal Service, United Way, USAA, Verizon, VISA, and The Walt Disney Company.

Jim Kouzes is the Dean's Executive Professor of Leadership, Leavey School of Business, at Santa Clara University. Not only is he a highly regarded leadership scholar and an experienced executive, but *The Wall Street Journal* has cited him as one of the twelve best executive educators in the United States. In 2006 Jim was presented with the Golden Gavel, the highest honor awarded by Toastmasters International. Jim served as president, CEO, and chairman of the Tom Peters Company from 1988 through 1999, and prior to that led the Executive Development Center at Santa Clara University (1981–1987). Jim founded the Joint Center for Human Services Development at San Jose State University (1972–1980) and was on the staff of the School of Social Work, University of Texas. His career in training and development began in 1969 when he conducted seminars for Community Action Agency staff and volunteers in the war on poverty effort. Following graduation from Michigan State University (B.A. degree with honors in political science), he served as a Peace Corps volunteer (1967–1969). Jim also received a certificate from San Jose State University's School of Business for completion of the internship in organization development. Jim can be reached at **jim@kouzes.com**.

Barry Posner is professor of leadership at Santa Clara University (Silicon Valley, California), where he has received numerous teaching and innovation awards and served as dean of the Leavey School of Business for twelve years (1996–2009). An internationally renowned scholar and educator, Barry is author or coauthor of more than a hundred research and practitioner-focused articles. He currently serves on the editorial review boards for *Leadership and Organizational Development*, *Leadership Review*, and *The International Journal of Servant-Leadership*. Barry is a warm and engaging conference speaker and dynamic workshop facilitator. Barry received his baccalaureate degree with honors from the University of California, Santa Barbara, in political science, his master's degree from The Ohio State University in public administration, and his doctoral degree from the University of Massachusetts, Amherst, in organizational behavior and administrative theory. Having consulted with a wide variety of public- and private-sector organizations around the globe, Barry currently sits on the board of director of EMQ Family First. He has served previously on the board of the American Institute of Architects (AIA), Junior Achievement of Silicon Valley and Monterey Bay, San Jose Repertory Theater, Public Allies, Big Brothers/Big Sisters of Santa Clara County, the Center for Excellence in Nonprofits, Sigma Phi Epsilon Fraternity, and several start-up companies. Barry can be reached at **bposner@scu.edu**.

Dan Schwab has more than twenty years of experience as a trainer, facilitator, and coach and has consistently made leadership development his passion and focus. From his first association with The Leadership Challenge® Workshop as a ropes course guide in 1989, to leading dozens of workshops in the last several years, Dan has brought skill and dedication to bear on helping others unleash their visions of the future. He is currently a Certified Master of The Leadership Challenge.

From 2001 to 2009, Dan served as director of training and organizational development for the Trust for Public Land (TPL), where his expertise in adult learning contributed to the success of one of America's most effective non-profit organizations. Prior to TPL, Dan worked as an internal training consultant with a multinational financial services firm and, as a consultant, designed and facilitated hundreds of learning programs for firms in Silicon Valley and across the United States.

A graduate of Dominican University of California, Dan holds a degree in human resource management, as well as a certificate in training and human resource development from the University of California, Berkeley. An intrepid community activist, outdoorsman, and world traveler, Dan lives in Richmond, California. He can be reached at **danjschwab@gmail.com**.